DESIGN AND MAKE
SLIPCOVERS

HEATHER LUKE

NEW HOLLAND

For Sarah, Jackie, Julie, Chris, Liz, Lucy, Helen, Judi, Lisa and Charlotte

———————

Published in the United States in 1998
by Sterling Publishing Co. Inc., 387 Park Avenue South,
New York, NY 10016

First published in the UK in 1997 by
New Holland (Publishers) Ltd
24 Nutford Place, London W1H 6DQ
United Kingdom

ISBN 1 85368 467 8 (pbk)

Managing Editor: Coral Walker
Photographer: John Freeman
Designed by: Grahame Dudley Associates
Illustrations: Claire Davies

Reproduction by CMYK Ltd, South Africa
Printed and bound in Singapore by
Tien Wah Press (Pte) Ltd
2 4 6 8 10 9 7 5 3 1

ACKNOWLEDGEMENTS
With thanks to the following fabric companies for their help:
Page 5 LeLievre; page 20 Bennison; page 24 Osborne and Little;
page 30 Bennison; page 35 Pierre Frey – rug, De La Cuona – shawl;
page 36 Pierre Frey – cushion, De La Cuona – shawl; page 37 Bennison;
page 41 Pierre Frey – bottom left; page 46 Bennison;
page 50 Percheron – toile de jouy; page 59 Titley and Marr;
page 60 Le Lievre – top right; page 71 Bennison and Pierre Frey.

My personal thanks to John Freeman for his dedicated photographs,
to Gillian, Coral and all those at New Holland who have carefully steered
this book from conception to birth. To the brilliant seamstresses from my team
past and present – Chris Amey, Julie Toop, Sarah Westcott, and Jackie Pullman
who made the slipcovers. And heartfelt appreciation from us all, to Dibby
Nethercott, Mary Stewart-Wilson, Elizabeth Peck, Carol Hicks, and Heather
Phelps-Brown for allowing us to photograph their lovely homes and without whose
support this book would certainly not have been possible.

CONTENTS

INTRODUCTION

Deliciously overdone, this fantastic weft-woven silk transforms an old bentwood chair into a dresser chair to be envied.

Casual, easy-clean, and adaptable – slipcovers are entirely acceptable in the home as the fashion in furnishings reflects the increased informality of clothing and other areas of lifestyle. Confusingly, a slipcover may be fitted or loose, or it can be draped. A cover can be made to fit so tightly that it will be indistinguishable from an upholstered cover. Alternatively, it can be loose enough to slip on and off, or even draped and styled to follow its own interpretation.

Your period of home and preferred style of furnishing will have the most influence, but fashion and furnishing trends should be considered so that your ideas are not quickly outdated. Watch particularly for trends in mixing colors and fabrics. Choose a tone slightly deeper than the main fabric for a formal cover, a soft tone with a floral pattern or self-piping for an informal cover, and a check or stripe on the bias for impact.

Just as warm, dark colors complement the atmosphere of short gray days, so light, airy furnishings reflect the long, light days. Here, slipcovers come into their own as several sets made in various colors and fabrics can be slipped on and off easily with each changing season.

Slipcover-making skills are not difficult to master. Each day I am lucky enough to see the transformation of old, outdated pieces of furniture into things of real beauty as a single flat length of fabric is cut, snipped, fitted, and stitched in the hands of an expert. And I am always amazed when teaching new students how quickly and accurately these skills can be learned and put into practice. Once the basics have been mastered and templates made, additional sets of covers can be made with the confidence of experience, and a first success will inspire you to more projects. But, slipcovers are an investment and the making should not be taken lightly either in time or expense. Buying inexpensive fabrics is always false economy – for all the work which you will put into your covers, they should serve you well. With fabric you really do get the quality for which you pay.

Try to obtain information about the "rub test" of any fabric which you intend to purchase. Most fabric companies rely on the Martindale test, in which a sample fabric is put into simulated normal use to clarify the extent of wear. A fabric rated 15,000 is suitable only for very occasionally used covers, whereas 60,000 would satisfy the most abused family sofa. A 35,000-40,000 classification will cover most general uses and will include many good-quality upholstery fabrics. However, for a piece of furniture experiencing minimum wear, don't reject stunningly beautiful drapery fabrics because they have a low grading.

Natural fibers are comfortable to work with and to use. Cotton, whether fine lawn or heavy velvet, makes and wears with impunity. Whether woven into stripes or checks, bobble weaves, terrycloth or damasks, knitted or printed, there are more slipcover fabrics available in cotton than can be imagined.

Linen union, which is a blend of cotton and linen fibers, is often hailed as the perfect slipcover fabric. It is good value for money, but in time the stronger threads cut into the weaker — rather as the harder of two gold rings will wear away the softer. One

hundred percent linen is the best to work with — easy to manipulate and seams finger-press like a dream — but the best linen is costly. Plain and inexpensive linens will show every fault and crease; so test a piece first. Printed linens are the most forgiving and good tempered: perfect for professionals and beginners alike.

I hope the selection of armchairs, sofas, small chairs, and stools shown within this book will inspire you to rummage through upholstery fabrics, and master the basic skills of slipcover making so that you can use my ideas to spark off your own.

BASIC TECHNIQUES

STITCHES

Always make sure you start and finish all stitching with a double stitch; never use a knot.

Herringbone stitch

Herringbone stitch is always used over any raw edge for lined covers or skirts that have hand-stitched hems.

Ladder stitch

Ladder stitch is used to join two folded edges invisibly together. Slide the needle along the fold ¼ inch and straight into the fold opposite. Slide along for ¼ inch

and back into the first fold, again directly opposite.

Slipstitch

This is used for hand-sewing gussets and plackets. Make each stitch approximately ⅜ inch long. Slide the needle through the fold for ⅜ inch and pick up two threads of the opposite fabric. Push the needle back into the main fabric exactly opposite and slide through for another ⅜ inch.

Buttonhole stitch

Used of course for buttonholes,

but also wherever a raw edge needs to be strengthened or finished. Work from left to right with the raw edge uppermost. Push the needle from the back to the front, approximately ⅛ inch below the edge. Twist the thread around the needle and pull the needle through, carefully

tightening the thread so it makes a knot right on the edge of the fabric to form a ridge.

Blanket stitch

Originally used to finish the raw

edges of wool blankets, its use is now mainly decorative. It is most comfortable worked from the side with the edge toward you.

Push the needle from the front to the back, about ¼ inch from the edge (this measurement will vary with large or small items). Hold the thread from the last stitch under the needle and pull up to make a loop on the edge.

Hemming stitch

Used for hemming unlined covers,

each stitch should be roughly ⅜ inch in length. Slide the needle through the folded hem, pick up two threads of the main fabric, and push the needle directly back into the fold.

PINNING

When pinning two layers of fabric together or piping to fabric, always use horizontal and vertical pins to keep the fabric in place from both directions.

The pins running parallel to the presser foot need to be removed just before the foot reaches them; the cross pins can remain in place, so that the fabrics are held together the whole time.

SEAMS

Flat seam
The most common and easiest seam for normal use. With right sides together, pin ⅜–¾ inch in

from the edges at 4-inch intervals. Pin cross pins halfway between each seam pin. These cross pins will remain in place while you are stitching to prevent the fabrics from slipping. Once machine-stitched, open the seam flat and press from the back. Press from the front. Now press from the back again, under each flap, to remove the pressed ridge line.

French seam
Use this seam for unlined fine cotton covers. Pin the fabrics together with the wrong sides facing. Stitch ¼ inch from the raw edges. Trim and turn the fabric over, bringing the right sides together. Pin again, ⅜ inch from the stitched edge and stitch along this line to enclose the raw edges. Press from the right side, always pressing the seam in one direction only.

Flat-fell seam
Use for heavier fabrics. Pin the

fabrics together with right sides facing and stitch ⅜–1¼ inches from the raw edges. Trim one seam to just under half. Fold the other over to enclose the raw edge. Press down. Stitch close to the fold line.

MITERED CORNERS

For a neat and professional finish, you will need to miter the hemmed corners of unlined

covers and skirts.
1. Press the side seam over and the hem up. Position a pin

through the point of the corner.
2. Open out the folds and turn in the corner at a 45° angle, with the pin at the center of the fold line.

3. Fold the hem up and the sides in again along the original fold lines. Keep the pin on the point and make sure the fabric is firmly tucked into the folded lines.

MAKING TIES

Ties are useful and decorative, and are used extensively for home furnishings, especially slipcovers.

Folded ties

Cut a strip of fabric four times the width of your finished tie and 1¼ inches longer.

Press one short end under by ⅜ inch. Press in half lengthwise, fold each side to the middle, press, fold, and stitch close to the folded edges.

Rouleau ties

Cut a strip of fabric four times the width of your finished tie and 1¼ inches longer. Fold in half lengthwise, right sides together, enclosing a piece of cord which is longer than the strip of fabric. Stitch along the short side to secure the cord firmly. If the rouleau is quite wide, knot the cord as well. Stitch along the length, ⅛ inch toward the raw edge from the center.

Trim the fabric across the corner, pull the cord through, at the same time turning the fabric right side out. Cut off the cord at the end. Press the raw edge under and slipstitch with small stitches.

PIPING AND CORDING

If piping or cording is to be used in straight lines, it will be easier to cut it straight. If it is to be bent around corners, then it should be cut on the bias. For ⅛-inch piping cord, cut 1½-inch wide strips. All seams should be made on the bias to minimize bulk when the fabric is folded.

To cut on the grain

Cut lengths as long as possible. Hold two strips, butting the ends together as if making a continuous length. Trim away both corners at a 45⁰ angle. Hold together and flip the top one over. Stitch where the two pieces cross.

To cut on the bias

With the fabric flat on the table, fold one bottom corner as if making a 12-inch square. Cut along the fold line. Mark pencil lines from this cut edge at 1½-inch intervals, and cut along these lines. Hold two pieces butting the ends together as if making a continuous strip. Flip the top one over and stitch together where the two fabrics cross.

Making and pinning

Press seams flat and cut away excess corners. Fold in half along the length and insert piping cord. Machine stitch to encase, approximately ⅛ inch from the cord. Keep the fabric folded exactly in half.

Always pin piping and cording so the raw edges of the piping or cording line up with those of the main fabric.

To bend cording around curves, clip the seam allowance for the cording to lie flat. For a right angle, stop pinning ⅝ inch from the corner, clip the cording right to the stitching line, fold the cording to 90⁰ and start pinning ⅝ inch in on the adjacent side.

Joining

To join piping or cording, overlap by approximately 2¼ inches. Unpick the casing on one side and cut away the cord so the two ends butt up. Fold the piping fabric across at a 45⁰ angle and cut along this fold. Fold under ⅜ inch and then pin before stitching.

BINDING

Binding one edge

1. Cut the binding strips to the

width required. Join the strips to make the required length.

2. Pin the binding to the fabric, right sides together, and stitch slightly less than ⅜ inch from the

raw edges.

3. Trim the raw edges to roughly ⅜ inch. Press from the front, pressing the binding away from the main fabric. Fold the binding to the back, measuring the edge to ⅜ inch, keeping the fabric tucked firmly into the fold, and then pin at 3¼-inch intervals. Turn to the back of the fabric and herring-bone-stitch the edge of the binding to the main fabric.

Binding a corner

Stop pinning short of the corner by the width of the finished binding. Fold binding back on itself to make a sharp angle and pin across this fold line. Pin on the adjacent side, the same distance from the edge. Stitch binding on, stopping at the pin, and secure. Begin stitching again at the same point on the adjacent side. Press to miter. Fold fabric to the back, mitering in the opposite direction.

PLACKET WITH TIES

1. Cut two pieces of fabric, one 3¼ inches and one 4¾ inches wide, and each the length of the opening. Stitch the widest one to the back and the narrower one to the side of the chair cover, along the ¾-inch seam allowance.

2. Starting with the back, press this wider flap to the front. Measure 1¼ inches from the seam line and fold under. Turn to the back, and fold under another 1¼ inches so the fold lines up with the stitching line on the back and pin. Press the side flap to the back and fold in half to make a hem.

3. Finish the hemline, whether a skirt will be attached, a binding skirt, or a self-hem. Slipstitch

along the folded lines with small stitches.

Pin the ties in place and insert with the first seam line. Add hooks and bars if you prefer.

INSERTING A ZIPPER

The first method is simple. The second is used for inserting a zipper into a corded seam.

Method 1

1. Pin one side of the zipper to the opening, ⅛ inch away from the teeth. Machine topstitch this half of the zipper in place.

2. Machine the other side of the opening to the zipper, forming a flap to cover the teeth.

Method 2

1. Apply cording to the front of the fabric. Join front and back

pieces, allowing a gap for zipper.

2. Pin one side of the zipper against the cording on the front of the cushion from the wrong side. Machine stitch tightly in place.

3. Open out cushion seam and pin other side of the zipper in place, making sure the fabric butts up to the cording without a gap. Machine stitch in place, stitching across ends of zipper to prevent the head becoming lost.

PREPARATION

This is the key to successful sewing. Prepare well, and the work should go smoothly, with few errors. Look at various factors before you begin: where you are going to work, what you plan to use, linings and interlinings. Here are some guidelines to bear in mind before you begin sewing.

For making slipcovers you will need:

Main fabric – as plan
Muslin to make a "toile" or pattern
Long-bladed, sharp scissors for cutting fabric
Short, sharp scissors
Long pins
Tape measure
Piping cord
½-inch fabric tape
Hooks for closure
Pins and needles

THE WORK TABLE

If possible, you should stake your claim on one room which can be put aside for your own use, even if it is only while you are making your covers.

A dining room or guest bedroom can be made into a temporary work room with little effort. A work table which is at least 4 x 8 feet and preferably 5 x 10 feet will make the whole job so much easier. You can buy a sheet of board in either of these sizes. Cover your dining table with thick felt so the board can be rested safely on top.

Alternatively, make some sturdy legs that can be bracketed to the underside of the board. This quickly made table can then be laid temporarily over a guest bed. The space below can be used to store all your fabrics, and the top will be wide enough for you to work on a whole width of fabric at a time. Pure luxury compared to hands and knees on the floor! The height of the work table should be whatever is comfortable for you; I use a table 38 inches high.

Cover the top with heavy inter-lining and then a layer of lining. Staple these to the underside; pulling the fabrics very taut as you go. You will now have a soft surface which is ideal for pinning and pressing.

CHECKING THE FABRIC

Before you begin to cut the fabric, check it thoroughly for flaws or incorporate them into parts that will not be seen, such as hems. If the fabric is badly flawed, return it.

Measure each length and mark it with pins to make sure you have the correct amount of fabric. Always double-check your measurements before you start to cut.

Fabric should ideally be cut along the grain and to the pattern, but sometimes the printing method allows the pattern to move off the grain. If necessary, let the pattern run out slightly to either side – but a ¾-inch run-off is the most you should tolerate.

PATTERN MATCHING

It is well worth spending a little time to make sure that all fabric patterns are matched correctly at the seam on each width.

1. Place one of the lengths of fabric right side up on the work table with the selvage facing you. Place the next length over the first, right side down. Fold over the selvage to reveal roughly ¼ inch of pattern and press lightly.

2. Match the pattern to the piece underneath, and pin through the fold line along the whole length. You may need to ease one of the sides at times – using more pins will help. Go back and place cross pins between each pin. Machine- or hand-stitch along the fold line, removing the straight pins and stitching over the cross pins.

3. Press the seam from the wrong side and then again from the front. Use a hot iron and press quickly. Turn the fabric over again to the back and press under the seam to remove the pressed ridges. If the background fabric is dark or you are using a woven fabric, snip into the selvages at 2-inch intervals. If the background fabric is light, trim the selvages back to ⅜ inch, removing any printed writing.

PLACING THE PATTERN

The pattern should be placed so that it always runs from top to bottom. For this reason the outside and inside arm pieces should never be cut as one. Patterns should run from the top of the inside arm to the seat and from the top of the outside arm toward the floor. Match all patterned or geometrc prints at each piping seam. Plan all pieces so that the pattern follows through up from the floor, across the seat, and up the back.

CUSHION PATTERNS

Cushions should always be made to match the position of the pattern on the main body of the sofa or chair cover. If possible, plan enough fabric to make all cushions reversible.

If you have made a paper template of the chair seat or stool, transfer this to muslin or scrap fabric and add ¾ inch all around for seams. If the cushions are square or rectangular, measure carefully and note the longest and widest measurements. Add ¾ inch all around for seam allowances. Measure gussets, ruffles, and piping, and note the sizes needed, adding seam allowances.

Plan these pieces (top, bottom, gusset, etc.) on the work table to see how they fit into the fabric width. If you are making several matching cushions, they must be planned thoughtfully to obtain maximum benefit from the fabric.

If the fabric has a dominant pattern, the pieces will need to be planned thoughtfully so that the cushions are cut together to prevent wastage of fabric.

On seat and back cushions, patterns should always read from front to back. The gusset should be placed so that the pattern follows through and matches exactly. Piping may be cut on the bias or on the straight; if there are any curves or curved corners, cut on the bias so that the piping can be bent and still lie flat.

As a general rule, allow 1 yard of fabric for each seat. So allow approximately 2¼ yards for a two-seat sofa.

Also allow for pattern repeats. Small geometric patterns and all-over designs need approximately 10 percent extra fabric; large prints may need almost double the amount a solid fabric will take to match up correctly. Fabric bindings need to be of similar weight to the main fabric, or try wide ribbon, linen tape, or upholstery webbing.

PLANNING FABRIC CUTS

Look at the chair or sofa you wish to cover and try to visualize it finished. Decide whether you prefer a solid or patterned fabric; whether a print or weave, whether the pattern should be large or small; where the piping lines should be; whether you want to define a particular line or "lose" another; whether the piping should be coordinated, contrasting, or as the main fabric; how formal the chair will be; whether the skirt should be ruffled, box pleated, corner pleated, fringed, etc.

View the chair as a series of rectangles, i.e. inside back; outside back; inside arm; outside arm; seat; front gusset; skirt; cushion pieces; arm cover. Measure the chair for each piece, allowing 1¼–1½ inches seam allowance in each direction, plus 4–8 inches for a tuck in. Push your hand down into the chair around the seat, the inside arm, and inside the wing to check the depth.

The tuck in should be as large as the space allows, as the farther the fabric can be pushed in, the less likely it is to pull out.

Seams should never be in the center of a cover. Always use a full fabric width at the center with panels joined at each side. Seams should follow from the front, across the seat, and up through the back.

PIPING

Piping cord is available commercially in a wide choice of thicknesses, graded numerically according to the diameter of the cord, corresponding roughly to the metric measurement of the diameter. So a ¼-inch cord is designated No. 5. No. 00 is the narrowest and No. 7 is the widest cord normally available.

Piping strips should be cut to make a ¾-inch seam after the fabric has been folded around the cord. Two-inch strips will fit No. 4 cord, which is the most generally used size.

Tiny pipings are used for decorative work and in places where piping is desirable but a thick edge of color is not. Chunky piping cords are used where a statement is needed and can be very effective as self piping, so that the size rather than a contrasting color makes the detail.

MEASURING AND PLANNING

ESTIMATING FOR AN ARMCHAIR

Plan your pieces (see right) on paper to make best use of the fabric width to estimate the amount needed. With a patterned fabric, it is best to mark the paper in sections to show the repeat and the pattern size. Cushions should be planned so that backs and fronts are the same and that each one is reversible or a mirror image of the other. The shape of the couch or chair will dictate the reversibility of cushions.

DINING OR SIDE CHAIR

Measure the chair at the widest and highest points, following this list as a guide.

Inside back	– width
	– length + tuck in
Outside back	– width
	– length to floor or top of skirt
Seat	– front width
	– back width
	– front to back + tuck-in
Skirt	– to floor
	– all around

Add 2¼ inches all around for seam allowances. Allow 6 inches for the tuck-in at the back of the seat, and 8 inches for the flap under the

Pieces to measure

Inside back	A – width		H – length over arm + tuck-in
	B – length+ tuck-in	Seat	I – width + tuck-in
Outside back	C – width		J – length + tuck-in
	D – length to skirt or floor	Front gusset	K – width
Outside arm	E – width, measure top and bottom		L – depth
		Front arm	M – height
	F – depth		N – width
Inside arm	G – width, measure top and bottom	Sides	O – around the frame
		Skirt	P – depth of skirt

Direction of pattern

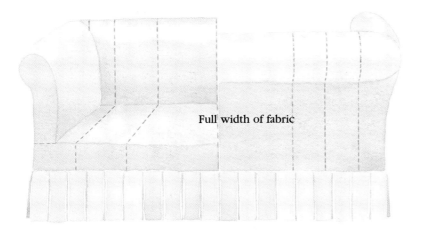

Full width of fabric

Full width of fabric

Seam positions

which is soft enough to fold and tears easily to fit around difficult leg and arm interruptions. A thick pencil is useful to mark the edges of the seat on to the paper, and tape will help hold the folds and tears in place. I then transfer this pattern to heavier brown paper from which I cut the fabric and form patterns.

Tape paper to the back, front,

and sides of the chair seat. Bend the paper along the shaped seat and draw the line with a thick pencil. Tear and fold the paper around the arms and legs to give a really accurate shape. Remember, you can always stick a bit of paper back on if you over-cut by accident. The important thing is to fit the paper accurately enough to make a precise template from which to cut your final pattern.

chair seat. Decide whether you want to have a skirt around the chair seat, and if so, the style and fullness. Also consider whether to have any other decoration.

Plan these pieces on graph paper to calculate the fabric needed. Make allowance for any pattern repeat and choose the pattern position on the chair back and seat.

CUTTING OUT

Cut out the pieces of fabric as planned. Use muslin if you are making a toile or cut straight into the top cover if you are confident. Make enough cording for the whole job.

Using the tape measure, place a vertical row of pins to mark the center line of the inside back, outside back, front, and seat.

WOODEN CHAIRS

Squab cushions add a decorative, welcoming touch to a wooden chair seat, but the primary

function is to make a hard chair seat more comfortable. Foam or rubberized hair with a batting wrap are the best padding solutions for this type of cushion.

You will need to cut a template from the chair seat itself to use as an accurate pattern for the seat shapes. Either paper or tightly woven cotton are suitable, but for this purpose, I prefer newspaper,

TAILORED COVERS

Good use was made of the printed fabric border. Instead of a skirt, flaps stitched to the border fabric between each leg have been tucked underneath and tied at each corner.

Slipcovers are an investment in time – first yours to make, then followed by years of use by family and friends. If you are an enthusiastic beginner, I would advise you to start your slip-cover career with a cover for a stool or a bedroom, kitchen, or garden chair. The worn-out couch in the living room might be your reason for starting on this road, but there are some useful principles to learn which might be less painful on a smaller subject, with less fabric at risk.

Of course, once you become really competent, you will have to hide your new-found light under the nearest bushel, or your services will be in great demand! Everyone wants to know a slipcover maker.

You will need to decide how tight or loose your slipcover should be. The best tight covers are hardly recognizable as slipcovers, fitting so snugly over upholstery that not a wrinkle can be seen. Excellent for formal-style sofas and chairs and traditional rooms, tight covers look upholstered but can be removed easily for laundering. Very baggy covers – slipcovers usually in light cotton or muslin – were originally dust covers, but are now highly fashion-able as summer coveralls for sofas and wooden chairs alike.

Slipcovers are normally easier to make if they are fitted tightly but made with some ease — so that a wobbly seam or an uneven cut is disguised. Overall patterns are sympathetic, disguising odd creases, whereas solid fabrics will show all discrepancies. Choose carefully to make life as easy as possible.

CUTTING THE COVER

Refer to pages 10-13 before you begin in earnest and practice with a toile if you are nervous. Slipcovers must always be fitted with the fabric pinned in place right side out, i.e. as it will look when finished. This is because not only are there never two chairs exactly the same, neither are the left and right sides of any one chair exactly the same!

1. Fold the inside back piece in half lengthwise, with the right sides of the fabric together. Finger-press lightly. Line up the fold line against the center line of the chair and pin at top and bottom. Open out the piece and pin at 4 to 8-inch intervals to anchor to the side and top of the chair. Pins should be at right angles to the chair with the points turned in. Repeat with the outside back, anchoring it to the sides and bottom of the chair frame as well.

2. Holding the fabric firmly between finger and thumb, pin the pieces together along the back edge of the chair. Remember that the pin line will be the seam/piping line. Pins should be in a straight line, nose to tail, right against the furniture to give an accurate line for stitching later. Start and finish 1½-2¼ inches above the arm on both sides. Pin from the back of the chair, and ease the front piece around shaped backs, making darts or small tucks at the corners.

3. Position the inside and outside arm pieces of one arm on the chair, checking the pattern is in the right place, and keeping the grain straight, vertically and horizontally. The pattern and grain of the outside arm should be level with the floor, not the top of the arm.

Pin these pieces together along the arm, making some allowance for any arm curvature. The seam may be at the top of the arm, on the outside of the arm or under the scroll, depending on the actual arm style of the chair. Repeat with the other arm.

4. Pin the arm fronts to the chair, checking that the grain is straight. Mark the position with two crossed pins. Anchor all around, with pins at right angles to the chair pointing in.

5. Pin the inside and outside arm pieces to the arm front, easing curves and fullness. Some arms will have no fullness to disperse; other arms will need one or two darts at this point, but the excess fabric will mainly be eased in with small gathers or pleats, spread evenly around the curved section.

6. Pin the outside arm pieces to the chair back piece. Joining the back arm to the inner back is the trickiest part, so should be practiced with spare muslin if you are a beginner. If you over-cut the seam, the cover will be too tight and if you under-cut, too loose. Fold the inside back piece up so that the fold line marks the seam from the top of the arm to the back. Fold the arm piece to make the opposite side of the seam.

7. Cut away the excess fabric to 1¼-1½ inch seam allowance as far as the start of the curve of the arm and the seat back (do not cut this too tightly yet in case some adjustment is needed). Make marking tacks with contrasting thread three or four times along the folds at exactly opposite points so the pieces can be matched accurately for seaming.

8. Pencil a line around the arm curve and down into the seat. Trim 1¼ inches away from this pencil line where there is no tuck-in space and approximately 4 inches where there is. Do the same with the inner arm. Either pin the fabrics together along the pencil line or fold each back on itself. The actual shape of the arm and the extent of the curve will make one of these methods easier than the other. Clip right into the seam allowances where necessary for the fabric to lie flat. Gradually cut the seam allowance back to ⅜ inch.

9. Trim the whole cover, leaving a ⅜-inch seam allowance all around. Cut V-shaped notches so that the pieces can be easily matched for stitching.

10. Stitch individual tailor tacks in contrasting thread to each piece at the actual meeting point of the arm seam with the arm front, and at any other area where they might be useful for matching the pieces before stitching. Repeat with the other arm.

11. Place the seat piece on the chair seat, again matching the center fold to the pinned line, and anchor all around.

12. Fold the two sides over along the length of the arms, so that the fold lines join the arm fronts at the edge of the front of the chair. Pin the front gusset to the front of the chair, checking that it is centered and level with the floor. Pin the top of this piece to the seat piece along the front edge. Where these two pieces meet the arm front, push a pin through all three pieces so that there is a definite point at which all pieces will meet when stitched. Mark each piece individually with a secure tack in contrasting thread at this point.

13. Pin the front gusset to the arm fronts, from the marked point to the bottom of both pieces. Measure and mark the folded back sides of the seat piece so that the tuck-in is equal from front to back along the length of the arm. Cut carefully along this line.

14. Pin the inside arm pieces to the seat piece for approximately 8 inches from the front toward the back, cutting back and shaping the meeting point to correspond with the available tuck-in allowance.

15. Using a wooden ruler, measure up from the floor all around to the skirt position. Mark with pins. Allow for the seam allowance and cut the excess fabric away. At this point, if the chair needs to have a back opening, fold back the outside arm piece and the back piece to allow for the necessary ease. Pin the fabric back on itself to keep the fold. Mark the top of the opening with a tack on each piece.

16. Tidy up and cut all seam allowances so that they are equal. (If you have accidentally under-cut at any point, mark the place, so that you can adjust the seam allowance to compensate when pinning the pieces together.) Make sure that you have snipped enough notches. Use single, double, and triple cuts to make matching easier. Remove the anchor pins and lift the cover off.

FINISHING

If you want the cover to be loose, you will need to stitch so that the seam allowance is less than that allowed, i.e. a stitched seam allowance of ⅝ inch of the ¾ inch allowed in cutting will give ⅛-inch ease on each side of the seam. It is usual to pin cording so that the front of the cord is on the seam allowance to give some ease.

The instructions have been given for a tight cover with the stitching line of the cording pinned along the seam allowance.

Make your own adjustments as you prefer, keeping them consistent throughout the assembly process. Always work with small areas at a time so a limited amount of the un-stitched cover is unpinned at any one time.

1. Take the pins from one of the seams joining the inside arm to the back. These seams are probably the most vulnerable to movement and fraying so they should be stitched and secured first. Turn inside out. Starting at the back, carefully match the tacks, and the ends of the easing cuts. Pin the seam down to the seat. Stitch, reinforcing the curve line by stitching two rows very close together. Do not be afraid to stitch right next to the cuts. If you give these too much berth, the cover will not fit back as well as it came off. Finish the seam. Repeat with the other side.

2. Next unpin one of the arm seams. If piping or cording is to be used on the seam, pin it to the right side of the outside arm piece. Stitch in place. Pin the inside arm to the piping line, right sides together, so the seam allowances and notches match. Stitch. Pin along the piping line and at right angles to it. The pins along the piping must be removed as the machine approaches, but the others can remain in place, preventing the two layers of fabric from "walking". Stitch in place as close to the piping as possible. Check from the front that the previous stitching line is not visible.

If you have used cording, pull the cord from inside the case at each end for ¾ inch. Cut the cord away so the casing lies flat beyond the point at which the back and arm front seam will cross. Finish the seam. Repeat with the other arm.

3. Unpin the front gusset. Turn inside out, pin the piping or cording along the gusset piece, and stitch. At the seam with the arm front, pull the cord from the piping ¾ inch. Cut away the cord so the case is flat beyond the tack mark. Pin the right side of the seat piece to the piping line, matching seam allowance and notches. Stitch the length of the piping, between the tack marks. Secure stitches firmly at each end. Finish this seam.

4. Unpin the sides of the seat from front to back. Turn inside out and pin together again, matching notches and seam allowance. Stitch from the front tack mark to the seam at the back.

5. Unpin one of the front arms. Turn inside out. Pin piping or cording all around the arm, to the right side of the fabric, snipping at ¾-inch intervals to ease around any curves. Make sure you have pinned the piping to give a good shape, and stitch. Pin the inside arm, outside arm, and the front gusset to the arm front, matching seam allowances and notches. Pin the arm seam so that it is pressed downward.

6. Ease any fullness carefully. Stitch from the bottom of the front gusset up to the point where it meets the seat. Finish with the needle in the tack mark. Secure with back and forth stitches to this point. Lift the cover away from the machine. Fold over the seam and start again, with the needle in the tack mark from the other side of the seam.

7. Stitch all around. Look at the stitching line from the front. You might find it quite hard to get close to the piping the first time, because of the joint difficulties of the curve and the fullness. Stitching a small section at a time, slowly stitch as close to the piping as you can, so that the previous stitching line is not visible from the front. Finish the seam. Repeat with other arm. Ease one fabric on to the other.

8. Repeat the same stitching process on the center back, remembering to stitch just a small amount at a time.

9. Unpin the back piece. Pin the piping to the right side of the fabric from just above each arm. Snip to ease where necessary and stitch in place.

10. Pin the front to the back piece along the piping line. Use plenty of pins, pinned at right angles to the piping to ease any fullness. At the top corners make sure that the hand-stitched or darted corners lie flat and that the finishing stitches are inside the seam allowance. Stitch as close to the piping as possible.

11. Slide the cover back on the chair. Check that the seam lines are good and re-stitch any that aren't satisfactory.

12. Check that the hemline is still straight and an even distance from the floor. Make the back opening placket if needed (see page 9). Make a skirt and stitch to the hemline. Stitch the end of the placket to enclose the raw edges at the end of the skirt. Attach hooks and bars or ties (see page 9).

13. Press all seams from the front over a damp cloth. Press the cover and ease it back on the chair. Make sure the seams all lie in the same direction. Ease the cover around curves and corners. Finger-press piping lines to straighten. You will need to spend time easing and fitting the cover into place to obtain the best fit.

Slipcovers transform a dining room chair: this bright check can easily be removed and cleaned.

SKIRTS

Although not essential, skirts or dust ruffles are most useful both to disguise poor legs and to alter the visual impact of a chair or sofa. In a room full of leggy side chairs and tables, skirts on one or two chairs or a single sofa can redress the balance and make the situation immediately more pleasing. This country-style chair with its distressed, blue-painted legs has been given a more comfortable appearance by the addition of a gently ruffled printed linen skirt. Always make the skirt separately and attach it to the otherwise finished cover.

DESIGN AND MAKE SLIPCOVERS

ASSEMBLY

Decide the depth you wish the skirt to be. Add seam allowances of ¾ inch for the top and 2¼ inches for the hem. Measure the sides, front, and back of the chair separately. Plan your skirt to fit the four sides. Corner-pleated skirts are arguably the most used, the simplest to make, and ideal for formal situations.

Corner-pleated skirt

1. Add 15¾ inches for the pleats at each corner. Allow 1⅜ inches to one back piece for the underlap if there is a back opening. Plan to cut each section so there are no visible seams. Sofa skirts will need to have seams on each side of the central width on the front and back sections, following those on the seat and outer back seams. It should be possible to hide all other seams inside the pleats at each corner.

Cut the lining to match. Seam the short sides and press flat. Stitch the lining and top fabric together along the length, ⅜ inch from the lower edge.

2. Press the seam toward the lining so fabric bulk is kept to a minimum. Press the main fabric over to the lining side by 1¼ inches. Pin together and press lightly from the front.

3. Handstitch the short ends. On the right side, measure and mark each side and each pleat. Pin pleats in position and baste to hold. Pin cording along the top edge. Stitch. Pull the cord away at each end and fold the raw ends in.

4. Stitch the skirt to the chair cover. If there is a back opening on the cover, first finish the raw ends at the top of the underlap by carefully slipstitching the bottom of the placket over.

Ruffled skirt

1. Add measurements of the four chair sides together and multiply by fullness required - usually two to two-and-a-half times. Add 2 inches for any underlap at the back. Divide figure by the fabric width, and cut widths required for this length. Cut lining the same depth and enough widths for same length.

2. Join seams and press flat. Pin main fabric and lining together along one long side. Stitch ⅜ inch from edge. Press hem 1½ inches to back. Pin together along top edge. Stitch a gathering thread ⅜ inch down. Divide length of skirt into eight and mark each section with a tailor's tack. Divide cover hem into eight sections and mark. Match marking tacks and ease gathers evenly. Stitch close to piping — two rows are probably needed to come close enough to cover first stitching line.

Binding the hem

1. Cut fabric strips four times the finished binding width, e.g. 2½ inches wide for a ⅝-inch bound edge. Cut skirt and lining fabrics plus ⅜ inch for a top seam allowance but not at bottom. Stitch lining to one long side and skirt fabric to the other, just over ½ inch from raw edges. Press both seams toward binding, and from the front to remove puckers.

2. Fold binding in half and press. Pin top of both fabrics together.

SKIRT SELECTION

When the couch or chair has been piped with an alternative fabric, whether a contrasting color, say blue and white, or a coordinating one such as deep pink on soft pink, or a complementary fabric such as a small check on a floral print, the same theme will continue to the skirt. Perhaps just one row of piping at the top will be all that is needed, but binding the hem serves to weight the skirt visually. Buttons with loops or buttonholes, snaps, ties, frogs, and many other dressmaking finishes can be used to decorate the corners of the skirts, as long as the method allows each skirt section to remain sharp at each corner.

Binding the hem might have a more practical use when, for example, the main fabric has a rose print on a light ground and the piping fabric is a deeper tone, as the deeper edge disguises dirt picked up from the floor.

1. Contrast piping and inset pleats make a simple corner-pleated skirt stylish.
2. Each skirt section is made up separately with the sides cut 4 inches longer at the front and back so these sections can overlap. Make rouleau loops and stitch at the end of the skirt between the top fabric and the lining. The contrast edgings and details are optional and, depending on the room style, can be sharply contrasting or gently coordinated.
3. Cut the skirt in one long length,

adding approximately 6¼ inches to gather around each corner — this is a softer alternative to a pleat.

4. A ruffled skirt gives a soft and homey finish to a country-style or casual couch. Contrasting binding and piping are not necessary, but can make all the difference. Choose middle-toned colors to go with patterned fabrics, a small print or stripe with a larger all-over print, or closely toned solid colors.

5. Knife-pleated skirts fill the gap between the informal, feminine dust ruffle and the formal, more masculine straight skirt. Allow three times the fullness and make each pleat so it starts right where the last finished. They are approximately 1½ inches wide. Plan them to fit exactly between two chair corners. This means that the pleat sizes might vary slightly on each side, but this should not be at all noticeable.

6. Box pleats are made in the same manner as knife pleats. Allow three times fullness, pleat each one against the next, and divide equally between the sides so that a chair corner always fits at the center of a pleat.

Box pleats, knife pleats, inverted pleats, and tapered pleats are traditional skirt finishes for both formal and informal situations. Formal rooms and severe furniture will require fewer, very tailored pleats; cottage-style furniture needs pleating to be informal, so smaller pleats which kick out playfully rather than standing side by side in strict rows are probably preferable.

4

5

6

DESIGN AND MAKE SLIPCOVERS

ARM SHAPES

It is rare to find two arms that are exactly the same size on an old armchair or sofa, and it is also often the case on a new one. Small differences on new arms are not easy to spot, but still each arm will need to be cut out separately.

The rounded club arm extending to a slight wing (left) shows one of the many and varied arm and side combinations which you might find. The importance of good straight piping lines, evenly spaced, is apparent.

Old arms will become mis-shapen with use over the years and almost always one arm has been flattened more than the other. Small upholstery repairs might be needed – a little re-padding and tightening of the top cover, for example – but much can be disguised by a well-thought-out and fitted slipcover.

Your priority must be to keep the piping lines that run the length of the arm very straight and positioned in the best place. It is difficult to give much direction on this because there are so many arm shapes. On a scroll arm, the seam could be almost at the top or right on the side (see below); on a club arm the seam should give a clear edge, and on a laid-back arm the seam could be along the most prominent edge or tucked down into the outside roll. Pin the two arm pieces together in several positions or alternatively draw pencil lines along the arm to help you visualize the options.

THE STRAIGHT ARM

The traditional straight arm or Victorian laid-back arm can both be treated in this way. A pinned and stitched dart is the preferred finish for a sharp corner, but if the arm is more rounded than this one, then controlled pleats can be a most attractive way to ease the fullness of the inside arm piece.

THE CLUB ARM

The club arm needs to have its form identified with very straight piping lines. The distance between the piping lines on the front arm and along the top arm must be measured accurately so the gusset takes priority in the fitting. Any lumps and bumps must be taken up in the side panels.

THE SCROLL ARM

Scroll arms can be fat or thin, short or tall, squidgy or firm. Use your eye to make a good front shape and allow the front piece to take priority in the fitting. To make a misshapen arm beautiful, stitch piping to the front arm piece first and then pin the sides to the defined line.

FINISHING
DETAILS

The decision whether to define the edges and outline of the sofa or chair or not is personal choice. Piping in some form is needed to give definition and to aid stitching, but self piping is quite enough if there is no need for any other decoration. Flat piping, cording, ruched braid, small pleats, or a tiny frilled edge are all plausible

alternatives for varying situations and fabric choices. For instance, velvet piping is difficult for a beginner to sew, so cording or ruching should be chosen.

1. Self piping gently defines the shape of the sofa or chair without making a conscious statement.

2. Cording might be flanged for stitching into, with the seam as fabric piping, or stitched in place afterward with a circular needle.

3. A plain contrast should be soft in tone if the room is subtly

decorated, but it can be a dramatic contrast in a bold room.

4. Large and small checks give a "now you see me now you don't" compromise between self piping and toned contrast.

5. Flat piping uses a piping strip but no cord. This is ideal for cushions in wicker or Lloyd Loom chairs.

6. Chunky piping in the same color and fabric, or of another texture, can make a statement on structured furniture.

DESIGN AND MAKE SLIPCOVERS

ARM COVERS

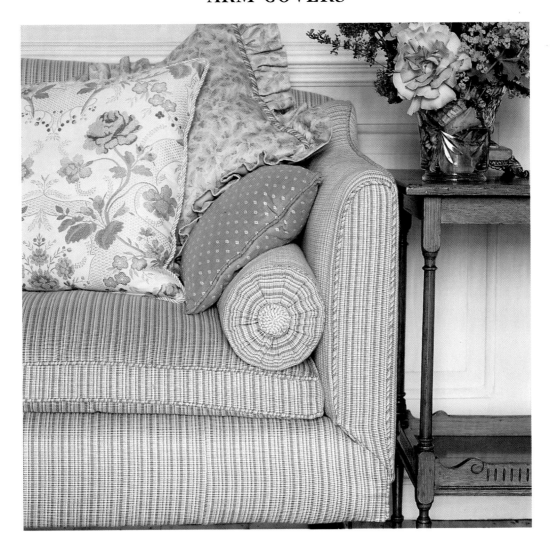

Arm covers are large affairs extending the length of the arm and long enough at each side to tuck right down behind the seat cushion and into the sofa, and to finish along the top of the skirt on the outside. This arm cover was truly invisible as the stripes of sofa and arm cover match perfectly. We had to push the arm cover to one side and position the camera carefully to be able to show how the bottom of the arm has been cut away to match the upholstery beneath.

Armcaps are shorter than the length of the arm and, although the inside will still tuck down beside the cushion, the outside will be cut away to finish along the arm approximately 4-6 inches down. On a scroll arm, the arm cover will be cut to snuggle into the recess.

ARM FINISHES

Slip-over covers or informal loose covers are more fashion-orientated and therefore provide more opportunity for decorative finishes and different shapes than tailored covers. These four ideas were cut on a scroll arm, but can be adapted to a club, straight, wing, or laid-back arm. With a T-shape cushion, the front skirt will need to return along the side to join the front panel.

1. Both the side and front fall straight to the floor. Contrasting fabric piping, a let-in flap, and covered button bring attention to the detail.

2. Self-piped seams allow the decorative buttons to take the attention. Rouleau loops, character buttons, elaborate frogs, ribbons, or toggles are some other ideas for a decorative closure.

3. Unpiped seams are perfect for the simplest, relaxed slip-over summer cover. Rouleau ties casually control the inset panel and outside edge. Stitch in place firmly to prevent restless fingers from destroying your creation.

4. Stitch a series of small contrasting ties to the outside edge and create a row of neatly tied bows to bring a touch of formality.

Top: A junk shop find, this simple kitchen chair becomes attractive and intensely practical with its new slipcover. Above: Accurate pattern matching is essential for a professional finish as are handsewn cotton bars for small restraining hooks.

Always cut arm covers with the finished cover on the chair so that accurate allowances for piping and exact pattern matching can be achieved. Plan, cut, and fit in the same way as you did to make the main cover. Full-sized arm covers are slipstitched to the back piping, seam, or opening, becoming virtually indistinguishable as separate pieces.

For cleaning, just unpick the stitches, launder, and re-stitch when almost dry. Armcaps are held in position with small stitched touch-and-close fasteners, hooks and stitched bars, or slip-covered pins.

1

2

3

4

ARM SHAPES

29

WINGS

The wing of an armchair or sofa, however small, usually needs to be cut quite separately from the rest of the cover.

1. Cut out pieces for the backs and arms as before. Pin the inner and outer chair backs together along the top of the chair. Pin each piece securely to the upholstery beneath. Cut and fit the arms.

2. For each wing, cut two squares, one for the inner and one for the outer side. Measure carefully – the distance between the back and front of the inner wing can be deceptive.

3. Pin each piece securely to the upholstery beneath, taking care to keep the grain straight. Use enough pins so the center line remains straight when pulled from both sides. Pin the pieces together around the front shaped edge, easing and snipping as necessary to make a good tight fit. Pin the length of the outside wing to the outside back.

4. Pin the inner wing and chair front pieces together at the top, making cuts and folding seam allowances as needed for the fabric to lie flat. Some wing chairs need the seam to angle back to the corner, but most will run straight from the point of tuck-in to ¾–1¼ inches from the outside corner.

5. Push your hands into the tuck-in gap (the space between the wing and the inside back) to see how deep it is and where to start and stop the tuck-in.

Left: A slipcover extends the invitation to sit comfortably in this substantial wing chair, which underneath is upholstered in a rather strict manner.

Above: Rather than a separate wing, a chair might have a winged side. Often, as here, the outer side is cut in one piece but the inner side will be cut in two pieces: one for the inside arm and one for the inside wing.

Pinning these together along the arm length allows any shaping and easing to be incorporated into a seam which can then be piped or corded for strength.

QUILTING

Straight skirts were desirable but would have been too formal for this room. To present a relaxed atmosphere, the covers were cut overlong and both skirts and boxed cushions lightly quilted. Coordinated piping adds definition without calling immediate attention.

Quilting has often been called upon to save the day if a fabric is prone to creasing with constant use. Often employed for bedcovers and sofa and chair cushions, quilting gives a "natural" creased effect which is much more attractive than the creasing that often occurs across cotton covers. Quilting can be used to create form, as geometric designs are imposed on a plain fabric, or "outline" quilting can identify a particular pattern.

Always cut fabric to be quilted 3-10 percent larger. Light quilting through one layer of curtain interlining or 2-ounce synthetic batting would need only 3 percent overcut. If you want to promote a design, then up to three layers of 4-ounce batting might be used.

To prepare panels for quilting, place each piece of backing, batting and top fabric together and baste securely all around. Baste along the center lines and then across to create quarters.

Quilt the cover or cushion panels before assembling, but after the first fitting. Measure and pin the lines to be stitched and mark with a fabric marking pencil or baste in a contrasting color. Hand or machine stitch through all layers, always starting from the same edge. Avoid puckers by holding the fabrics firmly at each side, and stitching slowly. Hand stitching will be slower, but there will be no danger of puckering and you can use heavier threads, jute string, yarn, and even decorative stitches.

CUSHIONS

Boxed, Turkish, and wrap-around cushions can be used together well if the styles of furniture are mixed compatibly.

Early couches were made with just one cushion on the seat, constructed of horsehair stitched into a mattress ticking cover. Although undoubtedly gaining a more comfortable resting place than the wooden or tightly upholstered seat beneath, by today's squashy feather/down/fiber combinations, this method of seating can only be considered extremely unwelcoming.

However, there are times when the style of a piece of furniture has to be more important than the comfort. In such cases, I have covered horsehair pads with either a down quilt or a wool pad, both of which become tolerably comfortable without spoiling the traditional lines.

The most comfortable and manageable fillings have a high proportion of down. A mix of 85 percent down with 15 percent curled feathers provides a beautifully soft filling which molds easily around the body, returning to shape almost as soon as you leave it. However, down is rare and expensive, and the fillings can become more costly than the couch.

Try to aim for a 60 percent down and 40 percent feather combination — or a less expensive but heavier 40 percent/60 percent down/feather. The generally offered 85 percent feather and 15 percent down is not really acceptable, as the cushions become flat very quickly and are then difficult to handle and heavy to lift as you try to pummel new life back in. If this sounds familiar and your cushions are fairly new, try removing about 30 percent of the feathers and replace them with down. If your pillow forms are old and heavy, the curled feathers will have degenerated into a flat, unresponsive form, incapable of holding any air, and the whole pad should be changed.

BOXED CUSHIONS

Boxed cushions are formal and traditional, but allow ample opportunity for detailed finish. Use contrasting fabrics for gussets or piping, stitch ruched braid, cords, or flat braid instead of piping. Apply decorative buttons, ties, rouleaux, or toggles for decorative closures. Quilting in any form, appliqué, and many other hand-worked finishes can be applied or stitched for an individual touch.

ASSEMBLY

1. Cut out the pieces and make cording following the instructions on page 8.

2. Place the top and bottom pieces flat on the work table, exactly together. Snip irregular marks on all four sides using single, double, and triple cuts at 4–8 inch intervals.

3. Starting on the back edge, pin cording to the right of the fabric, all around the top and bottom pieces. Pin so the stitching line will be on the seam allowance. At the corners, clip right up to stitching line on the cording, open out the cut so that the cording forms a tight corner. Pin securely. Join the cording as instructed on page 8.

Jacket tweeds make wonderful, hard-wearing cushions. Here, trimmed with leather, the overall effect with the silk paisley shawl and a touch of leopard skin is extremely chic.

4. Stitch on the cording. Insert the zipper into the gusset strip following the instructions that are given on page 9. Join to the other gusset piece.

5. Starting with the free end of the gusset, pin one side of the gusset to the top of the cover. Match the seam allowance and then pin it to the piping line. Cut into the corners, right up to the seam allowance, to give a good square corner.

6. Where the zipper gusset and the main gusset meet, pin together and stitch the short seam before finishing the pinning. Cut away any excess fabric. Stitch all around as close to the cording as possible. Check from the front that the first cording stitching line is not actually visible. If it is, stitch around again from the other side, making sure that your stitching line is inside the first one.

7. Pin the other side of the cover to the opposite side of the gusset. Start at the back and, matching the seam allowances, pin along the piping line. Match the notched marks by scoring a pin line from a notch on the stitched side, across the gusset, following the fabric grain. At each corner score a pin line from the stitched corner to the opposite side of the gusset to align the corners exactly. Snip into the seam allowance. This cut should form the corner. Stitch the cover all around.

8. Cut across the corners to within ¼ inch of the stitching. Finish the seam, open the zipper, and turn the cover right side out. Push each corner to a good shape with a point turner or the end of the scissors. Press all over. Lightly press the seam allowances away from the gusset. Fill the cover with the form, checking that the filling fits right into each corner.

TURKISH CUSHIONS

Turkish cushion covers, with their particular pleated or lightly gathered corners, fit over the same boxed pads but lend an informal air best suited to a country fabric or cover. The fronts and backs are cut to fit over the pad and meet along the center line of the gusset. The easiest way to make sure the corners are perfect is to fit the cover over the pillow form. Once the four sides are pinned, take up the corner excess with a single pleat, an inverted pleat, or a series of small gathers, depending how casual the finish is to be. Self-pipe or hand-stitch cord over the seam. Finish with a knot at each corner.

WRAPAROUND COVERS

Informal and easy-to-make cushion covers, suitable for the complete amateur and those frightened of piping, wraparound covers depend only on side gussets and a simple closure.

Cut one length of fabric from the center back gusset along the cushion length, under and around to meet at the center back. Allow ¾ inch at each end for the closure allowance. Cut the fabric to the cushion width plus ¾-inch seam allowance on each side. Pin it over the form and adjust the back closure seam for a good fit. Remember, the form is always approximately 10 percent larger than the finished cover, so fit the cushion into the chair seat to check the fit.

Cut a gusset for each side, the depth and length of the cushion side plus seam allowances. Pin the gussets along each side, keeping the back ends square but easing the fronts to make curved ends. Adjust until a good fit is obtained, trim seam allowances to ¾ inch, and mark at regular points with colored tailor's tacks. These will help you realign the pieces once the pins have been removed.

Insert a zipper or make a placket for hooks and bars or ties along the closure seam. Open up and pin the side gussets in place, making sure the ease at each gusset front is neat, and any marking tacks are matched. Stitch together, finish seams, and then turn right side out.

If you would like to pipe the side gussets, do so before pinning them back to the main cover.

Wraparound cushion covers with side gussets are informal and suit squashy country chairs and sofas. Useful also for window seats and Lloyd Loom-style chair seats, they are often buttoned.

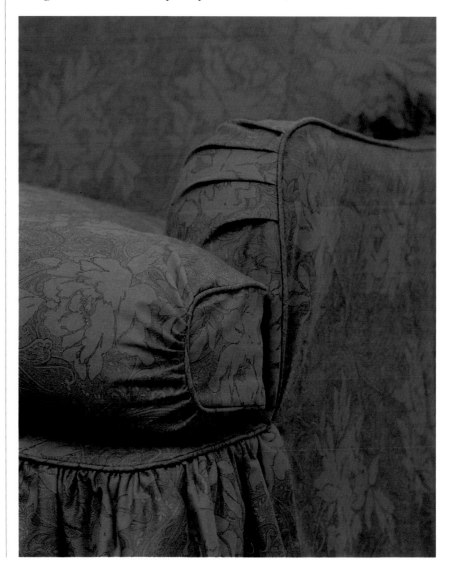

FINISHING DETAILS

Informal slipcovers or loose covers offer many opportunities for additional detailed decoration. Free from the restrictions of tailored cutting when form is imposed by the line of the furniture beneath, the shaping and cutting of informal covers can be quietly restrained or elaborate in the extreme. A keen slipcover maker might like to experiment with more complicated shaping and draping, reflecting details from couture garments.

Dimity print wallpaper is the backdrop to this charming medley of patterns which combines an antique Northumbrian quilt, monochrome roses, and a chic candy stripe.

A wooden kitchen chair can be transformed with a slipcover; by barely following the original shape, it can be given a character all its own. Armchair covers, too, can be made baggy and informal — especially useful if the shape below has deteriorated beyond that which a fitted cover could enhance.

Disproportionate or ugly chair legs can be conveniently disguised with a well-proportioned skirt. My preference is always to make deep skirts. I dislike the standard 6-inch variety generally on offer — too short a skirt can look "stuck on" and out of balance. Whether straight or gathered, I much prefer the effect and balance when a skirt hangs from the seat or from just below the front roll.

Buttons in any shape, form, texture, and size — toggles, frogs, ribbons, and braid — can all be successfully employed to maximize the individuality and character of different chairs.

DESIGN AND MAKE SLIPCOVERS

ARMCHAIR DETAILS

1. Gingham check from commercial suppliers is inexpensive and hard-wearing, being manufactured specifically for intensive hotel use and laundering.

Shaped to fit along the top roll and around the arms, the bottom and back were left loose for informality and easy removal. This chair in my kitchen suffers daily abuse from children and pets, but after constant washing and pressing, the cover still looks good.

Flat piping and the back ties are interesting details.

2. Although cut to fit the chair, a nursery cover needs to be casual and simple to slip on and off for cleaning. For ease, the arms were made slightly loose and the skirt ruffled from the seat. Nursery fabrics must be washable — I always think it is safer to pre-wash. Most fabrics will shrink a little in both directions, so don't just allow extra on the length. Remember also only to use pre-shrunk piping cords and to launder linings before cutting.

3. Another chair in the same nursery asked for a different treatment. Inset gussets at each corner have piped sides which spring out to give body and shape to the skirt hem. The cover was pinned to fit the chair as a tailored cover, but each seam was eased ⅜ inch before trimming.

4. Ticking is hard-wearing and available in interesting colors and varied stripes. Antique tickings from northern France, hand-woven cloths from Mediterranean islands, and other ethnic weaves are often tough enough to make good covers. Some tightly woven fabrics can be hard to pin and stitch. Also check out the creasing factor – crush a square in your hands and see how quickly creases fall out. Always pre-launder an unknown fabric.

5. This idea was taken from a favorite, old jacket — two fabrics with the same weight and fiber content cover an antique French chair whose velvet upholstery I did not wish to remove. Fabric-covered buttons and hand-stitched buttonholes reflect further details.

6. Playing with contrasting fabrics and turning stripes are part of the fun of making slipcovers. Center seams are essential in this chair to take up the back curve.

1

2

3

4

5

6

FINISHING DETAILS

WOOD FRAMES

Underneath, a show wood Louis XV sofa is in good repair having been recently upholstered in a traditional stripe. Ocher-dyed toile de jouy also makes a perfect slip-over cover for alternative use.

Couches, armchairs, garden chairs, kitchen, and dining chairs with wood frames are more difficult to slipcover than chairs which are fully upholstered. But, with a little more preparation, results are very satisfying, and slipcovers that just fit over them make pleasant seasonal or occasion alternatives. Wood-framed chairs sporting casual fabric covers suggest a softer and more relaxed atmosphere.

Covers cannot be pinned tightly enough to make fitted covers, as there will be pulls and creases which cannot easily be pinned out – problems which can only be mastered by an extremely experienced maker. So choose heavily textured fabrics and all-over patterns so that the overall shape of the cover is more important than the details and finishes. You can just see the striped fabric beneath, but this doesn't matter at all, given the change in formality which the slipcover has advanced.

All-white covers look tremendous in a summer house, but lightly colored fabrics and lightly printed patterns cannot be expected to hide fully the winter upholstery beneath. Only if the under-covers are really dark would I fit an unpiped muslin cover over the upholstery first.

Tailoring details can be incorporated most effectively to chair backs, and solid fabrics can be enriched from a structured treatment – if you have the experience and the will.

FINISHING

Slipcovers over wooden chairs are made in exactly the same way as for upholstered chairs. Fabric pieces are planned in the same manner. Each piece needs to be pinned to the chair for the fitting and then together along each seam line.

To make this possible, fabric lengths or woven tapes are used to bind the frame. Whether cane, metal, or wood, all frames are treated in the same way. On a free piece of wood, tapes can be tied around and knotted or pinned in place (see page 54). All tapes need to be tightly fixed, so that they do not swivel around as you pull on the fabric.

If the frame is old and tacky, you might be able to stick small pieces of woven tape to it, but if the upholstery meets the frame, tapes will need to be pinned to the upholstery on each side, stretched taut over the wood. You might be able to use tacks to hold the tape to the underside of the chair. But if all else fails, the chair will need to be bandaged from top to bottom and side to side.

For similar covers, make a seat template (see page 13) and cut two pieces of linen with a ⅝-inch seam allowance all around. Make two skirts, one to fit between the back legs and one for the rest of the seat.

Prepare piping (see page 8) and stitch to one of the seat pieces, ⅝ inch from the raw edges. Gather the skirts to fit and stitch to the seat along the piping stitching line. Pin rouleau ties to each side of the back legs, and stitch securely with several rows of a zigzag or backstitch. Place the other seat piece over, right sides together, enclosing all seams. Stitch together, leaving a small opening at the back. Finish seams, cut away corners, and clip curves. Turn out, press, and slipstitch the opening.

Right: Organza is draped over the chair and knotted at the back to add a frothiness which can be fun for some occasions.

Below: Seat covers for a set of antique French dining chairs protect the upholstery beneath. Crisp white linen launders easily, returning fresh time and again. An organdy border is stitched to the line with a decorative stitch in pearl cotton.

SINGLE CHAIRS

You can have fun with fabrics when covering single chairs. The chair on the right is covered with tailoring linen, which is finely woven with a lovely glaze which crackles a little when creased. A fitted back and seat give way to a fully gathered skirt with the cascade of pintucks stitched to the lower half. At the back, a center pleat punctuated with a hand-made ceramic button opens to show off the pintucked skirt.

On the left, an unfitted cover used to wrap a Victorian lady's balloon-backed chair was cut from a single length of fabric. Pin to the inside and outside back, and push as much as possible into the seat tuck-in to hold the fabric firmly in place. Pull the hanging flaps at each side to the back and pin together. Draw the curves around the seat front and on the floor at the back. Pin to check that the fabric hangs comfortably, then cut away. Bind all around with a complementary fabric.

A bow made from the same fabric as the binding was stitched to hold the ends at the center back.

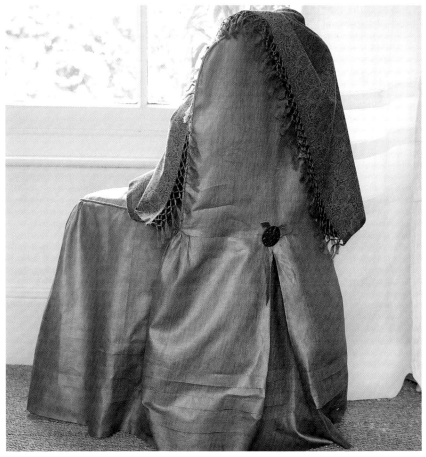

LLOYD LOOM CHAIRS

Genuine Lloyd Loom basket chairs crop up in antique or junk shops all over the world. Originally made in Britain, these chairs are small and light enough to transport easily and be useful in many situations. Copies and similar-style chairs are still being made fifty years later, as the Lloyd Loom style has found universal favor, used in bathroom, kitchen, bedroom, living room, guest bedroom, and even the dining room.

In various states of disrepair, Lloyd Looms are normally rejuvenated with a coat of paint and a new seat – a slipcover presents a plausible option.

MAKING UP

1. Plan the pieces to cut following the principles detailed on pages 12–13. Allow double fullness for the skirt. Cane or basket-type chairs have no place for pins, so bind the whole chair as if you are bandaging it; if the frame is already in poor repair, glue narrow tape around the edge.

2. Cut one piece of fabric for the inner back and seat and pin to the outside edge all around. Pin away the excess until the fabric lies completely flat against the seat back and on the seat.

3. Pin narrow binding tape around the raw edge to prevent the fabric from stretching.

4. Pin the skirt to the seat and back all around, taking up the fullness into pleats. These can be quite random, so don't spend too much time trying to make them all the same size. Trim back to leave a seam allowance of just under ¾ inch.

5. Make enough piping to fit all around the seat and back. Pin to each pleat. Carefully unpin the pleated skirt and stitch the piping to hold the pleats in place. Stitch the seat seams, and then stitch the inner back and seat piece to the piping. Refit the cover to the chair and mark the hemline. Stitch with a double row of machine stitches ¼ inches apart.

DAY BEDS

Strong ticking stripes from Normandy in a traditional brown and cream combine perfectly with toile de jouy printed with scenes from *La dame du Lac* in its original coloring. The day bed could be fully slipcovered or, as here, partly slipcovered with skirts on either side of the seat.

Attractively designed day beds can quickly be turned into temporary or permanent seating with the addition of covers and throw pillows. Day beds can be entirely slipcovered, perhaps in warm, sensuous fabrics: choose from damasks in wool, silk, or cotton, tapestries, velvets, wools, tartans, and plaids in plain and multi-colors. Or select simple fresh stripes, checks, crisp linens, or even filmy ethereal fabrics such as organdy, voile, and linen scrims.

Very fine open weave linen scrim would look marvelous over these painted bed ends, tied at the sides, but loose enough for the colors and pattern to show through. Or full covers can completely transform a bed with plain or poor-quality head and foot boards.

To fit the covers, the frame needs to be first bound with woven tape or lengths of fabric to provide an anchor for the pins (see page 54). Short skirts enhance the shape and character of wooden day bed frames. If you want to use filmy fabrics, a gathered skirt behind the side rails would be most appropriate.

A hint of the frame style should always remain – whether it is glimpsed through an open-weave cover or peeps through cutout shapes.

KITCHEN AND DINING CHAIRS

I favor simple checks purchased from a hotel supplier for my farmhouse kitchen. Sure that these commercial fabrics have been manufactured specifically for hard wear and frequent laundering, I can leave them in place whatever the age and number of family and guests eating with us.

Every country in the world has its own indigenous style of kitchen chair, most made of wood but some wicker or cane. Whether French, Dutch, Scandinavian, English, North American, Greek, Italian, Spanish, each evokes a definite style in the mind's eye if used as a description of an ordinary wooden chair. Unfortunately, although lovely to look at, many of them are uncomfortable to sit on for any period of time, as the chair seats are usually constructed from wood or woven rushes.

As life becomes less formal, many of us now entertain so much more in the kitchen – morning coffee, a glass of wine after work, or family suppers. Because of this, some sort of comfortable seat pad becomes essential. Squab cushions are flat pieces of foam or stitched hair, made to fit the seat shape, covered in fabric, and tied to the legs at the back of the chair. They can be made as simply or as decoratively as you prefer, and may themselves have slip-over covers for use on different occasions.

Kitchen chairs may also be entirely or partially slipcovered. I now keep several sets of covers to cope with many occasions, from a children's party, to Christmas, summer supper or winter drinks. Once you have made an initial pattern and have practiced on the first set, each additional cover takes only a short while to make – a set can be easily completed within a day or in a couple of evenings.

     DESIGN AND MAKE SLIPCOVERS

ASSEMBLY

Plan the amount of fabric needed following the same principles for all slipcovers (see pages 12–13) and use muslin to make the templates. You will find that wood-framed chairs need to be bound with lengths of fabric to provide an anchor for pinning.

1. Stitch tapes tightly in place to stop swiveling — pinned fabrics pull against each other. Thumbtacks can hold tapes on old frames. Tape can be used, but may remove paint.

2. For a seat template, pin some muslin to the taped edges. Push a pencil into the fabric around the back legs and cut muslin to shape. Draw around chair seat's edge and cut fabric along line. Check that the template is anchored and follows the seat shape. Put a note on the muslin to add seam allowances.

3. Cutting the back is a little more difficult if you have not made enough pinning points. (This cover should fall loosely, but the template cover must fit quite tightly.) The front and back pieces at the top of the chair must be pinned together close to the frame and the fabric at each side must be equal. Trim seams to ¾ inch and make notches and tailor's tacks to assist you when stitching pieces together — always mark any ease. Cut around the seat without seam allowances, but cut a ⅜-inch seam allowance for the back and front piece - note it in pencil on the template.

4. Cut out fabric pieces for the inner back, outer back, seat skirt, and two plackets. Add seam allowances where necessary. This skirt was cut 8 inches long to allow 1½ inches for the hem and ¾ inch for the seam allowance. Make flat piping. Cut fabric strips on the bias 2 inches wide and press in half.

5. Stitch the inner back to the seat and finish the seam. Pin flat piping to the outer back all around, making small tucks at the top corners, and stitch in place. Pin the inner back to the stitching line and ease or pleat the fullness around the top. Stitch flat piping around the seat and along the hemline of the outer back. To make the skirts, make ⅜-inch double hems to finish. Stitch gathering threads along the top, pull up, and pin to the seat and back, distributing the gathers evenly.

6. Make ties (see page 8) — four or six for each side. Pin one 1¼ inches below the top opening, one at the top of the skirt, and one in between if needed. Make a placket (see page 9) and pin it over the ties. As you stitch the placket in place, triple stitch back and forth over the ties to hold them securely in place.

The seam joining the seat to the inner back should fit snugly against the wood. Flat piping, cut on the bias, between the seat and the skirt makes an attractive finish.

A placket stitched around the back opening encloses all raw edges and secures the fabric ties.

Long tapes need to be stitched to the inner back/seat seam and tied to each chair back strut to prevent the seat from moving. You can just see the ticking squab which sits on the seat under the slipcover.

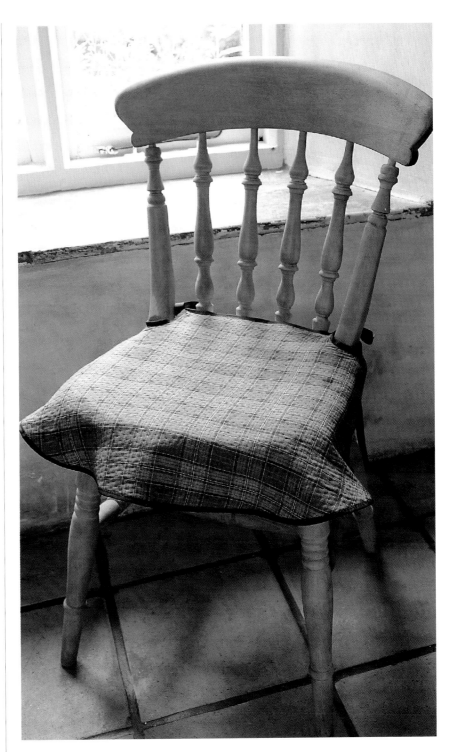

This simple cover reminds me of a horse blanket – reversible, easy to store when not in use, and very simple to make. Place the seat template on the fabric and cut around the back with no allowance for seams. Add 5 inches to the sides and front, following the curves and shape of the template. Stitch grosgrain ribbon or bias binding all around and make ties for the back legs to secure the cover to the seat.

CREATING A DINING SET

Once you have cut the first pattern and completed your first covers, you might be inspired to make more sets for other occasions.

Instead of making a separate ruffled skirt, add 7 inches to the outer back length and around the three sides of the seat template. A stenciled design can be painted on each piece before stitching them together. Use fabric paints, dry and press under a clean cloth with a hot iron. A simple hem was stitched all around and the back openings stitched together. Fabric-covered buttons stenciled with a miniature grape design hold small pleats at both legs.

For a tailored fit (above), the back was cut into three panels, shaped to take up the fullness. The two pleats were created by leaving the back seams open beyond the seat. Pretty stenciled-fabric buttons define the pleats and punctuate the plain cream.

To make a back opening (right), the outer back template is cut through the center and 3¼ inches is added to both sides. Instead of the ruffled skirt, add 7 inches to the length. Also add 7 inches to three sides of the seat template. Make the outer back first. Press extra fabric under, ¾ inch from center back line. Finish raw edges. Pin together two layers, lining up centers and over-lapping by 1½ inches. Make buttonholes on top piece and stitch covered buttonholes on under piece.

Assemble the cover as before, stitching the backs to the hem.

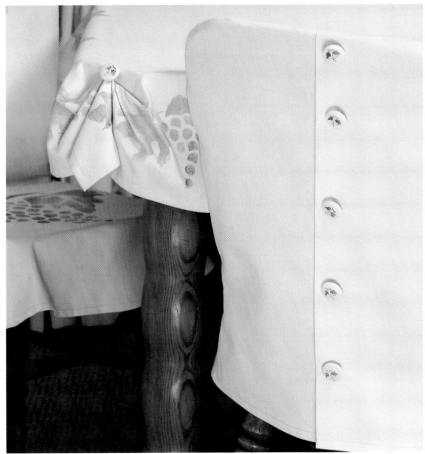

FORMAL DINING CHAIRS

Dining chairs usually have comfortable upholstered seats, and antique chairs especially are ideal for a premium fabric. These types of chairs need only a little fabric, which generally is seen rather than used. However, unavoidable spills will demand that a practical fabric should be considered.

Putting slipcovers on dining chairs is a good solution as slip-on covers can be permanent or temporary features. They can be removed to launder, or put on and off for dinner parties and Sunday lunch. Costly upholstery fabrics are then saved from damage and should last as long as the upholstery underneath.

The most comfortable dining chairs to accommodate our rather informal way of life and extended seating at table are not antique, but new and fully upholstered. These can be ordered upholstered in your own fabric or in muslin with removable slipcovers. In any case, more than one set of covers can transform your dining room for any situation. Richly colored Highland plaid fitted covers are excellent for the colder seasons, while blue and white stripes loosely fitted and held together with ties are excellent spring and summer furnishings.

A Highland plaid in rich blues and reds, threaded with olive green, covers soft caramel upholstery for the Christmas period. The addition of red ties and piping is warm and seasonal.

DESIGN AND MAKE SLIPCOVERS

SEAT COVERS

Often side chairs and carvers have backs and arms which interrupt the flow of a skirt. The only solution is to make as many skirt sections as needed, with flaps at each end to button over each other. Neat, precise cutting and finishing is essential for a pleasing result, so should only be tackled by an experienced stitcher.

On the chair on the left, as in many others, the back of the chair has been designed and made to join the seat. The back skirt panel has to be made as a completely separate piece, held only by the rows of buttons at each side.

Top right: A remnant showing ladies in Provençe regional dress was not quite large enough to cover this side chair. The solution was to seam it with a jolly red and white check around the ruffle. Long ties laced around the back legs keep the cover securely in place.

Bottom right: Simple, biblike covers can be quickly made and easily removed for laundering. Make a template of the chair seat and add 4¾ inches all around. At the back corner, keep the cutouts, using them to make the flaps which button around the legs. Hem or line the cover. Tack a cord around to hold the "bib" in place and knot at the front corners to gather up excess fabric.

ASSEMBLY

To make slipcovers for a set of upholstered dining chairs or a single desk chair, first measure, plan, and cut fabric pieces as shown on pages 12–13. You will need to decide your preferred skirt style and then follow the instructions and ideas on pages 22-23 for assembly. You will also need to make enough piping to finish the whole chair.

The basic principles are the same as for an upholstered armchair or sofa, so read these through carefully before starting and refer to them as necessary (see pages 16–19).

If the cover is to be lined, cut the lining pieces and baste to the top fabric, assembling as one piece.

1. Pin the inner and outer back pieces to the chair, placing the fabric center fold against the pinned center line of the chair and keeping the grain straight. Anchor to the outer edge all around. Pin these two pieces together, following the back line, tightly to the chair back.

2. Make a dart at the top corners and ease any fullness from the front curve. Fit so that the pins are lying nose to tail and the fabric is completely pucker-free. Cut the seat piece and place over. Pin the two pieces together as shown, marking the side seams and cutting an allowance for the tuck-in between seat and back.

3. Trim all excess fabric down to ¾ inch and make notches to assist you in matching the two pieces once the pins have been removed. Mark the seam around the seat with colored tailor's tacks to match it up again easily.

4. For a skirt starting at the seat's bottom, make front darts, and trim fabric to ¾ inch below the frame.

5. If your skirt is to start from the seat line, then draw around seat edge and cut to shape with a ⅝-inch seam allowance. Measure from seam line at top of seat, or the bottom of the upholstery to the floor, to find finished skirt length.

6. Remove pinned cover. Make any darts at the top corners and the seat front. Join seam between the inner back and seat. Pin piping around outer back and stitch, clipping to ease around shaping and to make a sharp corner.

7. Pin inner back to outer back, easing as needed, and stitch inside the piping stitching line. Check right side to see if first stitching line shows. If it does, stitch around again close to piping, until piping is neat and even. Pipe around seat if not already piped. Finish seams.

Dining chair backs are seen as much as fronts around a table. The scope for decoration is limited only by time and fabric choice.

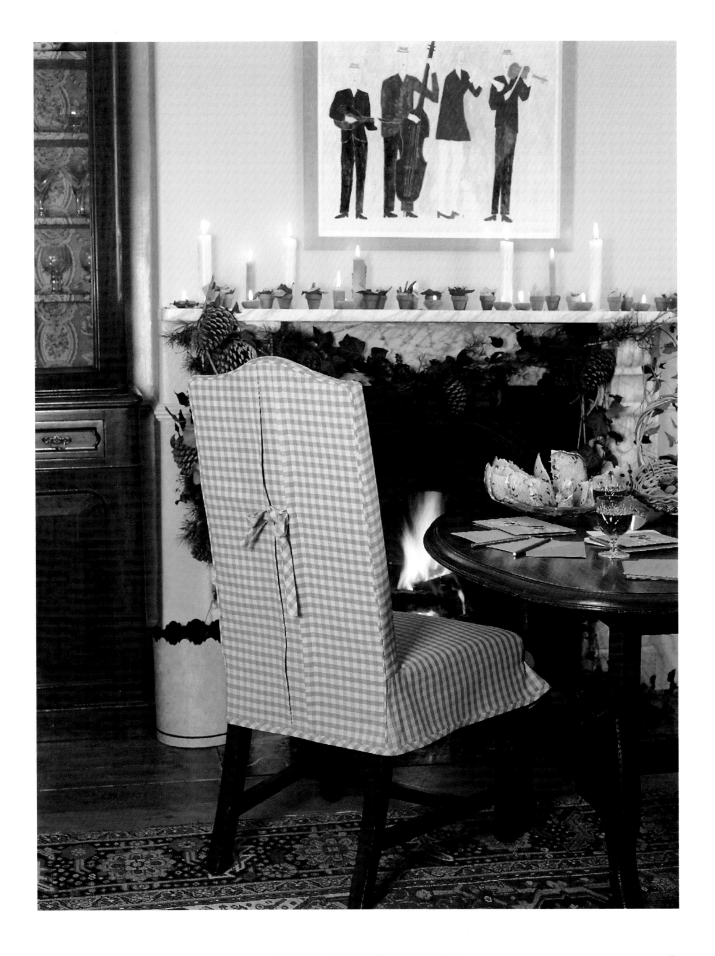

GARDEN CHAIRS

White linen piqué might appear at first to be impractical, but I always find white extremely good tempered, as it is the only color which can be washed at boiling point to remove drink and grass stains and, if all else fails, bleached and starched to perfection.

Garden chairs are inexpensive to purchase, easy to store, and light to transport, making excellent seating for additional guests, in kitchens, bathrooms, nurseries, dormitories, on camping trips, or picnics as well as for outdoor entertaining. However, they cannot all be described as attractive. In any case, a simple slipcover over part or the whole will transform these multi-use chairs completely.

Choose fabrics that are hardwearing and inexpensive. Check how much your chosen fabric will crease before purchase. Just scrunch a small piece in one hand and see how quickly the creases fall out. Garden chair covers will require constant laundering, but ironing is best kept to a minimum.

Full covers are cut following the same principles as all slipcovers and specifically for wood-framed chairs (see pages 42-49). Cut in only five pieces, outer back, inner back, seat, front, and two sides. Stitch together with simple flat seams and hem all around.

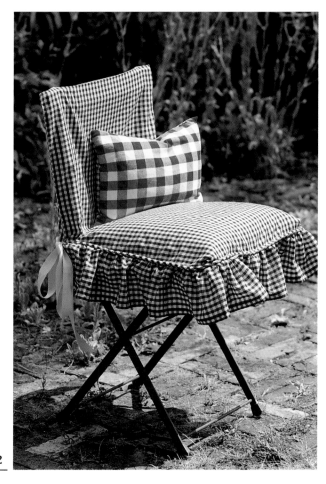

1

2

GARDEN GALLERY

1. Quilted padded covers in bright café cloth instantly dress these chairs in picnic mood. Cut two pieces of fabric long enough to cover the outside and inside backs and the seat length, with enough overlap to pad the back of the knees. Measure the chair's widest part and use this for the width. Add 5 percent for quilting shrinkage and ⅜ inch all around for seam allowance. Make a long strip of binding to fit all around, cut on the bias. Press this binding in half and stitch it to the front of the top cover piece, ⅜ inch from the raw edges. Place the back piece over with right sides together and stitch around three

sides, leaving one short edge to pull the cover to the right side. Stitch a length of heavyweight batting to the whole piece using the same seam allowance. Trim seams, turn and press, slipstitch the opening.

Plan three squares for quilting the seat and backs. Stitch through all layers so the covers are completely reversible. Slip it on the chair and mark the tie positions. Insert eyelets and thread matching fabric or tape ties through.

2. To add a little more comfort for a lingering summer lunch, I wanted a cover that would be attractive and disguise any scatter cushion that had been slipped on the chair seat.

The inner and outer backs are

cut in one length, and stitched from the top to the seat on both sides. Cut the seat piece to fit over a plump pillow, making tucks at each front corner and cutting around the back legs. Leave approximately 3 inches to slip down behind the pillow at the back of the chair. Ties will be stitched to this flap to hold the cover to the chair seat to prevent the pillow from sliding forward.

Pipe around the seat and along the bottom of the back piece. Make two skirt pieces with double hems stitched and gathered up to about twice fullness to fit along the back and around the seat. Stitch to the piping just inside the last stitching line. Finish all seams and raw edges and stitch ties to the inside back. Stitch matching fabric to the two back seams for decoration and tie into generous bows or loops.

3. These simple seat and back covers can be adapted to fit most chairs. Contrast solid fabrics with checks, florals, and stripes.

Make a template of the seat size and cut a piece of ⅜-inch thick foam to this pattern. For each seat, cut two fabric pieces, adding ⅝ inch all around to allow the foam pad to slide in, and 3–6 inches along the sides and front, for the skirt. Cut any shaping and allow ⅝ inch for each seam. With right sides together, stitch around three sides and the length of the skirts on the back edge. Turn out, press, place the

foam pad on it, and mark the position. Stitch around three sides to keep the pad in place, insert the pad, and slipstitch the back closed. Mark the position for the ties and make eyelets to hold the seat cover to the chair back.

4. This is a simple chair cover to make. Only two seams are needed or none if you use extra-wide fabric. Think of each section as a square, the outer back, inner back, seat, front skirt, and two side skirts. The back, the seat, and the front skirt are cut in one piece, with the two side skirts joined to the seat. Take one measurement from the floor at the back up to the top of the chair, down to the seat, across the seat, and down to the floor at the front. Cut fabric

the width of the chair plus 3¼ inches and the measured length plus 3¼ inches. Mark the top of the chair, back, and front and back of the seat section with pins or tailor's tacks. Cut two side skirts, with 3¼ inches extra width and 2¼ inches extra length. If the chair seat slopes backward, trim the top to fit since these pieces will not be quite square. Stitch the top of each side skirt between the marked back and front seat section, placing the skirts so that the seams are 1¼ inches in from each side. Make double hems all around using the 2¼ inches allowed on the sides and the 1½ inches for the hems. Attach ties to hold the cover at the back and front legs.

ASSEMBLY

1. These covers fit over two inexpensive director's chairs. Cut a template from muslin or an old sheet first to help you plan the center seam and arm facings. Cut the outer back the width of the chair plus 1½ inches for seam allowances on each side and hem and ¾ inch at the top. Cut one piece long enough to cover the inner back, seat, and to the floor, the width of the chair plus 3 inches at each side, ¾ inch at the top, and 1½ inches at the hem.

2. Cut two pieces for the inner arms, adding 8 inches to the front edge, and two pieces for the outer arms the width of the arms plus 1½ inches at each side.

From each of the main fabrics, cut one side of the inner back and seat, one side of the outer back, one inner arm, and one outer arm. Also make four ties, following the color scheme here if you wish.

3. Join the center seams of the inner and outer backs. Press flat and topstitch. Join the inner and outer arm pieces and finish in the same manner.

4. Pin the inner and outer backs together at the top of the chair, from above each arm, making a pleat on the front piece at the top corner. Remove and stitch seam.

5. Place the arm pieces over, with the flaps of the inner arm at the front. Pin the inner arm to the seat and inner back. Remove cover and make seams. Make ¾-inch double hems all around the raw edges. Fit cover back on and pin the positions of the ties. Double stitch these in place.

6. Inside the cover, stitch lengths of tape to the seat seams. They will tie around the chair arms and legs to prevent the cover from slipping.

Full covers completely disguise rather uninteresting plastic chairs. Skirts cut to finish 1–2 inches off the floor won't pick up moisture from the ground. Pink and white stripes look stunning in evening light for outdoor suppers.

STOOLS

The simplest cover is a square or rectangle tied to fit snugly over the stool beneath. Hems may be finished with braid or other decoration, corners rounded, and rouleau ties, cords or, as here, plaited suede used to hold the cover in place decoratively.

Stools are such useful small accessories in any living room, providing valuable additional seating for a small guest or family member at busy times. If firmly upholstered, a stool can be pressed into service as a spare table and perhaps as a center coffee table when necessary. As a foot rest placed in front of an armchair, a stool can extend the use to a day bed, providing welcome rest at the close of a busy day or to a house-bound patient. Tucked into a corner, placed in front of bookshelves, beside a fireplace, or in a cupboard when not in use, stools are no trouble to accommodate, being easy to maneuver to the point of need.

As with all slipcovers, stool covers may be tailored and fitted or loose, buttoned or tied, and held at each corner. Tailored covers follow the shape of the stool, usually with a skirt and often with a gusset at the top which helps to keep the cover in place.

Slipcovers are chosen for practicality or camouflage. Choose your fabrics carefully to perform the necessary function well. Washable fabrics need to be selected for hard-wear areas such as nurseries; heavy textured fabrics are best to disguise a battered item. Stools can successfully be made from old boxes with a little padding mounted on the lid.

The simplest stool covers are squares or rectangles thrown over and tied at each corner. Piped, bound, lined, unlined, buttoned, tied or laced, the fabric mix and detail of finish are limited only by time and imagination.

FITTED STOOL COVERS

Fitted stool covers benefit from the inclusion of a gusset of some depth to hold the cover firmly over the top cushion. A skirt can then be attached to reach the floor or, if the legs are good, just long enough to cover the upholstery.

If the stool design suggests just a top and skirt, stitch tapes into each corner long enough to tie underneath, so preventing the cover from sliding around.

ASSEMBLY

1. Measure, plan, and cut the top, gusset, and skirt pieces following the principles on pages 12-13. Make the skirt (see page 21), marking each corner clearly.

Make enough piping to fit twice around the stool. Place the top piece on the work table and pin the piping around. Keep the corners square and join neatly following the instructions on page 21.

Always plan and design any cover to suit your fabric. These boxed pleats have been placed to do full justice to both small and large teddies.

2. Stitch in place. Pin the gusset to the piping line, clipping into the corners sharply, keeping the fabric flat to either side. Join the gusset seam. Stitch along the piping stitching line. Check from the right side to make sure that the first stitching line does not show and if it does, stitch around again closer to the piping.

3. Stitch the remaining piping to the bottom of the gusset. Pin the skirt on and baste securely.

4. Fit the cover on the stool to make sure the length is correct. Stitch close to the piping and again if any stitches still show from the front of the cover.

UNFITTED STOOL COVERS

Squares or rectangles tied, buttoned, or knotted over the stool are effective, inexpensive, simple to make and practical to launder. Use fabrics that work with your other furnishings: scarves, small throws or blankets, lap rugs, or even antique floor rugs are all highly suitable and can be pressed into use.

1. The simplest stool cover ever made – measure from just below the upholstery, over the top to the same distance below the upholstery on the other side. Cut one square or rectangle to these measurements plus seam allowances for the top cover and one for the lining. Using an equal amount of fabric (here to match the sofa cover) gives opportunity to make changes.

Place the two fabrics together, right sides together, and stitch all around, leaving a 6-inch opening. Trim corners, pull right side out, press, and slipstitch to close the gap. Fit over the stool and stitch buttons to hold the corner pleats. Just remove the buttons for laundering.

2. Linen printed with roses is lined in a stylish cotton stripe, which also binds the hemline. As it is cut on the bias it adds an extra dimension. Rouleau ties hold each corner, and pleats are encouraged to fall informally. As an interesting alternative, fabric-covered buttons and tiny rouleau loops hold the chair skirt firmly behind.

1

2

3

3. This cover has been made reversible with a plain linen lining and decorative binding continuing to the other side. Also cut as a square or rectangle, the corners were then cut away to allow for the stool legs. The top and lining fabrics were placed together with wrong sides in and bound with fabric cut on the bias 2¼ inches wide (see page 9). To hold the cover in place, rouleau ties were laced through brass eyelets and crisscrossed down each leg.

DRAPED COVERS

A rose stitched from pink silk nestles in apricot bows, twisted easily from organdy ribbon — blissful for a summer christening party.

A single length of cotton organdy was draped over the back of the chair (right) and pinned so that the front just covered the seat and frame. At the back an extra 12 inches was allowed for the pintucks. The two spare corners at the front were pulled to the back of the chair and tied together. The folds and gathers that appear need to be pinned in place to look as natural as possible. Although these pleats should look uncontrived, if there were not some restraint, they would fall out each time the chair was moved.

The curved hem from center back to seat front might need to be cut to shape — just trim away the two corners.

Remove the organdy cover. Stitch the pintucks and make hems all around. Replace the organdy and secure the back pleats with safety pins or small stitches. Tie the corners over these fasteners and add decoration to suit the occasion.

Any soft fabric could be substituted - bright red silk for Christmas, pale pink for a christening, a silver or gold print to celebrate a wedding anniversary.

ASSEMBLY

1. Take measurements and plan cuts as pages 12–13. For this cover, the inner and outer back pieces are cut as one, with 20 inches extra allowed at each side. The inner and outer arm pieces are also cut as one, with 16 inches extra allowed at the front arm and 8 inches at the back. The seat piece is extended at the front and sides to fall to the floor.

2. Make Turkish or wrap-around cushion covers. Make four bows each about 3 x 8 inches.

3. Join seams as necessary and pin the back and seat pieces to the sofa. Pin together along the back tuck-in. Cut away at the arm front so that the side falls straight. Pin the hem in place along the floor. Trim the fabric along the seat/arm seam so only 4¾ inches remain — this for the side tuck-in.

4. Pin the arm piece in place along the top of the sofa arm, and smooth down the inner arm to the seat tuck-in. Pin together along the tuck-in.

5. At the back of the outside arm, pin the flap to the back of the sofa. Pin the back and arm pieces together to shape around the arm. This area needs to be cut well enough that the arm and back fabrics lie comfortably, but the particular fitting needed for a tight cover is not necessary.

6. Stitch the tuck-ins and arm/back seam together. Finish the seams. Fit the cover back on the sofa. Shape the excess fabric at the front arm so the hemline drapes into a gentle curve to the floor. Gather the back pieces together and cut the hemline to drape softly. Remove the cover again and hem these and all other raw edges. Press thoroughly and fit the cover back on the sofa.

7. Gather the fullness of each drape and stitch with double thread to hold. The flap which is at the back of each side should be pinned to the sofa back with upholstery pins, allowing the folds to hang over the back opening. Stitch rouleau bows over the gathering stitching.

Silk — spun and woven in the manner of linen — is convincing with its crunchy texture and matte finish, and is given away only by the extravagantly soft drapes. Fresh green revives the deep tan inner cover for spring and summer use.

DRESSING UP

Wonderfully informal covers can be made from simple throws or antique bed linen. Or for unusual shapes, make a simple cover customized to shape.

To make a draped cover as shown at the top, measure the couch and plan and cut the fabric pieces as pages 12–13. Include an extra 8–16 inches at each end. Pin to the couch, and join the seams of inside and outside backs, arms, and tuck-ins around the seat. Fit the cover back on the sofa, pin up the hems, and stitch. Gather up the excess at each corner, hand stitch, and finish with bows, ties, buttons, or rose details.

Antique linen sheets make perfect squares for tied chair covers. Worn areas can be cut away, patched, hidden in folds, or at worst, covered by a strategically placed cushion. In the picture on the right a new hand-embroidered sheet has been used with the beautiful stitchery taking pride of place. Just drape the sheet over the chair, even up the front and side hems, and push the excess fabric into the seat sides and back. If the cover drapes on to the floor at the back, trim it away and hem. Alternatively, fold under and baste if you want to preserve the original size.

CLEANING

To wash your slipcover, follow the manufacturer's directions for the fabric and half dry as recommended. Press carefully. Press into the seams from each side with the point of the iron. Do not press over the seams as they will usually contain at least four layers of fabric and will mark the main cover with a ridge.

Slide it back on the chair while still damp. Finger-press all seams in the same direction (usually to the back and down, although sometimes the shape of the chair demands otherwise). Pull cover into shape over curves and corners while still damp.

Press the cover while on the chair if needed. To press the skirt after the cover has been fitted, plug your iron into a socket positioned close to the chair. Make a plain cotton pad and place it on a low stool, lift up the skirt piece by piece, and press.

GLOSSARY

FIBERS

Acrylic Manmade from petroleum, often mixed with more expensive fibers to keep the cost down. Not particularly hardwearing.
Cotton A natural fiber, cotton is very versatile, woven, knitted, and mixed with other fibers. It will lose strength in direct sunlight, so protect. Soft, strong, easy to launder, washable if preshrunk.
Linen Fibers found inside the stalks of the flax plant are woven to make linen cloth in almost any weight. Distinctive slub weave from very fine linen to a heavy upholstery weight. A very strong fiber which is easy to work and will take high temperatures.
Silk From the cocoon of the silkworm, silk is soft and luxurious to touch. Fades in sunlight, so protect. Available in every weight.
Wool A natural fiber, liable to excessive shrinkage as there are scales on each fiber that overlap, harden, and mat up. Warm to touch and initially resists damp.
Viscose Wood pulp woven into fibers that mix well with other fibers helping them to take dyes and fireproofing. Washable and sheds dirt easily.

FABRICS

Brocade Traditionally woven fabric using silk, cotton, wool, or mixed fibers, on a jacquard loom, in a multi- or self-colored floral design. Some are washable, but most will need dry cleaning.
Cambric Closely woven plain-weave fabric from linen or cotton with a sheen on one side. Use, wash, and press as Muslin.
Canvas Plain-weave cotton in various weights. Available as unbleached, coarse cotton or finely woven and dyed in strong colors.
Chintz Cotton fabric with Eastern design using flowers and birds, often with a resin finish which gives a characteristic sheen or polish and which also repels dirt. The glaze will eventually wash out, so dry clean only. Avoid using steam to press and never fold or the glaze will crack.
Corduroy A strong fabric woven to form vertical ribs by floating extra yarn across which is then cut to make the pile. Press on a velvet pinboard while damp.
Crewel Plain or hopsack woven, natural cotton background embroidered in chain stitch in plain cream, wool, or multicolored yarn. Soft but heavy; may be washed, but test a small piece first.
Damask A jacquard fabric first woven in Damascus with satin floats on a warp satin background in cotton, silk, wool, and mixed fibers in various weights. Use the reverse side if a matte finish is **required**.

Gingham Plain-weave fabric with equal-width stripes of white plus one color in both warp and weft threads, producing blocks of checks or stripes, usually in 100 percent cotton. Mix with floral patterns or other checks/stripes.
Holland Firm, hardwearing fabric made from cotton or linen stiffened with oil or shellac.
Muslin Coarse, plain-weave cotton in cream or white with natural flecks in it. Available in many widths and weights. Wash before use to shrink and press damp.
Organdy The very finest cotton fabric with an acid finish that gives it a unique crispness. Wash and press while damp.
Organza Similar to organdy and made of silk, polyester, or viscose. Use layers of varying tones or pastel colors over each other.
Provençal prints Small-print designs printed by hand on fine cotton. Washable, hardwearing, soft, and easy to work with.
Tartan plaids Authentic tartans belong to individual Scottish clans and are woven or worsted fine twill weave with an elaborate checked design. Traditional wool plaid tartans are hardwearing.
Ticking Characteristic original herringbone weave in black and white, now woven in many colors and weights. Not usually pre-shrunk.
Toile de jouy Pastoral designs in one color printed on muslin using copperplate printing.
Tweed Wool or worsted cloth in square or rectangular checked designs in few colors.
Velvet Originally 100 percent silk, now made from cotton, viscose, or other manmade fibers. Woven with a warp pile and additional yarn in loops to form a pile. Care needs to be taken when sewing or the fabrics will "walk". Press on a velvet pinboard. Dry clean carefully. Always buy good-quality velvet with a dense pile which will not pull out easily.

INDEX

A
Arm caps 27, 28
Armchairs 24, 25, 26, 31, 38, 39
  club 24
  covering 14-19
  details on 40-41
  estimating fabric for 12
Arm covers 27, 28
  cutting 27
Arm shapes 24-31
  club 25, 28
  finishing details for 26
  laid back 25, 28
  scroll 25, 28
  straight 25, 28

B
Balloon-back chair 47
Binding techniques 9, 21
Blanket stitch 6
Bows 28, 29, 46
Boxed cushions 36
Box pleats 23
Buttonhole stitch 6
Buttons 38

C
Carver chair 61
Chairs 13, 14
  balloon-back 47
  carver 61
  desk 62
  dining 13, 56-63
  director's 68
  dresser table 4
  garden 64-69
  kitchen 13, 28, 38, 52-55
  Lloyd Loom 37, 48-49
    measuring and planning for 11, 12, 13
  nursery 40
  plastic 68
  winged 30, 31
  wooden 13, 38, 52-56
  wood-framed 42-49, 62-63
  see also armchairs
Chair seat, making template for 13
Cleaning slipcovers 79
Club arm 25, 28
Club armchair 24
Color schemes 4, 22
Corner-pleated skirt 21, 22
Cotton fabric 5
Couch, see sofa
Cushion fillings 34
Cushions 12
  boxed 34
  making 12, 34-37
  patterns for 11, 13
  squab 13, 52, 55
  Turkish 34, 37
  wrap-around 34
Cutting out 12
  planning for 11, 12, 13

D
Day beds 50-51
Desk chair 62
Dining chairs 13, 56-63
Director's chair 68
Draped covers 4, 74-78
Dresser chair 4

E
Equipment 10

F
Fabrics
  checking 10
  choosing 5
  cutting out 11, 12
Fillings for cushions 34
Finishing details 38-41
Flat-fell seam 7
Flat seam 7
Folded ties 8
French seam 7

G
Garden chairs 64-69
Gingham check 40
Graph paper 12
Gussets 6

H
Hemming 6
Hemming stitch 6
Herringbone stitch 6
Hook and bar closure 9

K
Kitchen chairs 13, 28, 38, 52-55
Knife-pleated skirt 23

L
Ladder stitch
Laid back arm 25, 28
Let-in flap 28, 29
Lined covers, sewing 6
Linen 5
Linen piqué 64
Linen union 5
Lloyd Loom chairs 37, 48-49

M
Martindale test 5
Measuring 12, 13
Mitred corners 7
Muslin 11, 12

N
Nursery chair 40

O
Organdy 44, 74
Organza 44, 45

P
Pattern matching 10
Patterns 10, 11, 12
Pinning 7
Plackets 6, 9, 55
Planning 12
Plastic chairs 68
Piping 11, 25, 26
  making 8

Q
Quilting 32, 33, 66

R
Raw edges, finishing 6
Rouleau ties 8, 28, 29
Rub test 5
Ruffled skirt 21, 23

S
Scroll arm 25, 28
Seams
  flat 7
  flat fell 7
  French 7
  self-piped 28, 29
Silk 4, 76
Skirts 20-23, 38
  binding hem 21, 22
  corner-pleated 21
  knife-pleated 23
  ruffled 21, 23
  stitches for 6, 7
slipstitch 6
Sofas 14, 27, 34
  covering 16-19
  planning covers for 11
Squab cushions 13, 52, 55
Stencil designs 57
Stitches
  blanket 6
  buttonhole 6
  hemming 6
  herringbone 6
  ladder 6
  slip 6
Stools 70-73
  fitted covers for 72
  unfitted covers for 73
Straight arm 25, 28

T
Tailored covers 14-19
  cutting out 16-17
  making 18-19
Tailoring details 42
Tailoring linen 46
Ticking 40, 41
Ties
  folded 8
  making 8
  rouleau 8, 28, 29
Toile 12
Turkish cushions 37

U
Unlined covers, sewing 6, 7
Upholstered furniture, covering 14-41, 61, 62

V
Velvet 5

W
Wing chairs 30, 31
Wooden chairs 13, 38, 52-56
Wood-framed chairs 42-49, 62-63
Work table 10
Wrap-around cushion covers 34

Z
Zipper, inserting 9